HJ.

Brimming with creative inspiration, how-to projects, and useful information to enrich your everyday life, Quarto Knows is a favourite destination for those pursuing their interests and passions. Visit our site and dig deeper with our books into your area of interest: Quarto Creates, Quarto Cooks, Quarto Homes, Quarto Lives, Quarto Drives, Quarto Explores, Quarto Gifts, or Quarto Kids.

Text © 2021 Zoë Tucker
Illustrations © 2021 Amanda Quartey

First published in 2021 by Wide Eyed Editions, an imprint of The Quarto Group. The Old Brewery, 6 Blundell Street, London N7 9BH, United Kingdom. T (0)20 7700 6700 F (0)20 7700 8066
www.QuartoKnows.com

A catalogue record for this book is available from the British Library.

ISBN 978-0-7112-6383-3

The illustrations were created digitally
Set in Lelo
Published by Georgia Amson-Bradshaw
Designed by Zoë Tucker
Production by Dawn Cameron
Manufactured in Guangdong, China, TT072021

9 8 7 6 5 4 3 2 1

FOR QUINN
AND ISAAC
- Z.T.

FOR MY GRANDMA,
PATIENCE NAA
LAMILEY MILLS
- A.Q.

JOURNEY
INTO
DEEP SP

NASA

written by
Zoë Tucker

WE ARE THE
NASA SCIENTISTS

illustrated by
Amanda Quartey

WIDE EYED EDITIONS

Mary was a mathematician at the Space Agency in America. She was part of an all-Black women's team and they spent their days solving long and tricky sums. Mary was like a human computer!

At that time, laws called segregation said that Black people and white people couldn't work together or use the same things as each other.

One day, Mary was asked to help out in a different department working with white people. Her day began as normal...

...but after a while, she needed to use the bathroom.

The other women looked at her, and laughed.

Mary's face felt hot as she rushed
from the room. She was furious!
There wasn't a bathroom for Black
women in the whole building.
She would have to hurry...

She was in such a hurry, she bumped straight into an engineer called Kaz. His papers spilled everywhere!

Kaz worked in the Supersonic Wind Tunnel. His job was to test different aircraft at super-fast speeds to make sure they were safe to fly.

Mary and Kaz got to work right away
and they made a great team!

She loved maths and solving
problems and he loved sharing
his ideas and knowledge.

One day, Kaz asked Mary to help him in the Supersonic Wind Tunnel. She was really excited and a little bit nervous.

There were hundreds of dials and buttons at the control panel. It was a lot to learn, but Kaz explained everything carefully.

They turned it on and the big fans roared into life!

Then Kaz showed Mary how to set up an aircraft for testing,

WOW! IT'S VERY LOUD!

and they measured and recorded everything.

This was cutting-edge engineering work that would help astronauts reach the Moon. It was very exciting!

Sometimes Mary helped the engineers with their maths problems.

One day, the head honcho of the team, a man called Mr. Becker, asked Mary to solve an especially tricky calculation.

Mary wanted to prove herself and impress Mr. Becker so she worked quickly and carefully.

When she was finished she double AND triple-checked her numbers just to be sure.

But when she showed the answer to Mr. Becker he said

IT'S WRONG!

Mary was confused.
She was sure it was right.

Mary and Kaz checked
the numbers again,

and then she spotted
the mistake.

Her sums were right, but the
numbers Mr. Becker had given her
in the first place were wrong!

Mr. Becker was mortified.
Kaz was absolutely right about Mary – she was brilliant.
He quickly apologised and everyone congratulated her.

Working with Kaz had taught Mary a lot about aerodynamics – which is how to make things go really, really fast!

The Soap Box Derby was coming and her son Levi wanted to enter. They began drawing out their ideas for his race car.

It needed to be super light, and super quick.

They built a magnificent car, with rocket ship fins and flames down the side. Levi couldn't wait for race day!

And all their hard work paid off. Levi whizzed across the finish line, ahead of everyone else. His supersonic soap box was the fastest in town!

But, there weren't many classes for women, and especially not Black women. It was frustrating and unfair. Mary didn't want to give up on her dream, so that night she talked to her husband, and they made a plan...

She found a class at a school for
whites only, which she wouldn't be allowed
to attend without special permission.
Determined to make her dreams come
true, she went to court.

COURT
HOUSE

Mary waited anxiously as the judge made his decision.

QUIET PLEASE
COURT IN SESSION

At last, the judge agreed and Mary won her case!

In 1958, Mary became the first Black female engineer in the Space Agency.

Mary and Kaz were part of a team
that sent astronauts to the Moon.
It took lots of people to make
it happen!

The engineers built and
tested the rockets,

and the scientists
built computers to
help fly them.

Then the mathematicians
checked all the sums to make sure
the astronauts really could get to the
Moon and back home again.

When the astronauts finally landed on the Moon in 1969, Mary and Kaz were proud to have been part of the special mission,

and Mary won an award for her important work on the project.

The friends worked together for many years, and when it was time for Kaz to leave, Mary threw him a big party.

Mary spent much of her life fighting for equal opportunities. She spoke at schools, and universities all over America about her work at the Space Agency.

Seeing everything Mary had achieved was inspiring! She encouraged people, no matter who they were, to reach for their dreams – just as Kaz had done for her all those years before.

WE ARE THE
NASA SCIENTISTS

Mary Jackson: April 9 1921 – Feb 11 2005

Kazimierz Czarnecki: 1916 (Poland) – January 30 2005

MARY AND KAZ became friends during a time when racism and segregation laws were in place in the United States. At the time, it was unusual for a Black woman and a white man to be friends, and the world around them certainly didn't make it easy for them.

There were rules that stopped Black people having the same things as white people. They stopped Black people from being able to vote and forced them to use separate shops, restaurants, water fountains and bathrooms. Black children even had to study separately, in a different school. It wasn't fair and it wasn't equal.

Mary and Kaz didn't allow the colour of their skin get in the way of their amazing friendship! The day they met at NASA changed both their lives forever and they worked together for the next 30 years. Throughout this time they always supported one another, pushing each other to be the best that they could be.

Kaz was inspired by Mary's love of maths and physics. He could see that she was a strong, intelligent woman. Together they co-wrote many reports on their discoveries in the Supersonic Wind Tunnel. Working alongside Kaz encouraged Mary to keep learning and to push through the barriers in front of her.

The 1950s and 60s were an exciting time to be working at NASA. America wanted to be the first country in the world to send a person to the Moon and everyone had to work really hard to make it happen. Mary and Kaz looked at the effects of supersonic wind speeds checking to make sure that each spacecraft could stand up to the journey into space. It was important work, and helped the crew of Apollo 11 make their journey to the Moon. They helped to make history.

Mary continued to achieve great things. With the support of her family and her friend Kaz, she fought for equality. She knew that other talented women like herself were also being held back by a lack of opportunity and encouragement. She dedicated much of her life to supporting young people and encouraging them to take an interest in science, just like her. Her legacy paved the way for hundreds of women behind her.